DISPATCH

The Lexi Rudnitsky Editor's Choice Award is given annually to a poetry collection by a writer who has published at least one previous book of poems. Along with the Lexi Rudnitsky First Book Prize in Poetry, it is a collaboration of Persea Books and the Lexi Rudnitsky Poetry Project. Entry guidelines for both awards are available on Persea's website (www.perseabooks.com).

Lexi Rudnitsky (1972–2005) grew up outside of Boston, and studied at Brown University and Columbia University. Her own poems exhibit both a playful love of language and a fierce conscience. Her writing appeared in *The Antioch Review, Columbia: A Journal of Literature and Art, The Nation, The New Yorker, The Paris Review, Pequod*, and *The Western Humanities Review*. In 2004, she won the Milton Kessler Memorial Prize for Poetry from *Harpur Palate*.

Lexi died suddenly in 2005, just months after the birth of her first child and the acceptance for publication of her first book of poems, *A Doorless Knocking into Night* (Mid-List Press, 2006). The Lexi Rudnitsky book prizes were created to memorialize her by promoting the type of poet and poetry in which she so spiritedly believed.

Previous winners of the Lexi Rudnitsky Editor's Choice Award:

2017   Gary Young, *That's What I Thought*

2016   Heather Derr-Smith, *Thrust*

2015   Shane McCrae *The Animal Too Big to Kill*

2014   Caki Wilkinson, *The Wynona Stone Poems*

2013   Michael White, *Vermeer in Hell*

2012   Mitchell L. H. Douglas, *blak al-febet*

2011   Amy Newman, *Dear Editor*

DISPATCH

POEMS

CAMERON AWKWARD-RICH

A KAREN & MICHAEL BRAZILLER BOOK
PERSEA BOOKS / NEW YORK

3 1350 00386 1426

Persea Books, Inc.
90 Broad Street
New York, New York 10004

Library of Congress Cataloging-in-Publication Data

Names: Awkward-Rich, Cameron, author.
Title: Dispatch : poems / Cameron Awkward-Rich.
    Description: New York : A Karen & Michael Braziller Book/Persea Books, [2019] |
    Summary: "Set against a media environment that saturates even our most intimate
    spaces, these poems grapple with news of violence in the United States today and in the
    past-in particular, violence inflicted on people of color and on transgendered people.
    Winner of the 2018 Lexi Rudnitsky Editor's Choice Award, Dispatch is poignant example
    of poetry's possibilities for transformation, solidarity, and renewal"—
Provided by publisher.
Identifiers: LCCN 2019028365 | ISBN 9780892555031 (paperback ; acid free paper)
Classification: LCC PS3601.W58 A6 2019 | DDC 811/.6—dc23
LC record available at https://lccn.loc.gov/2019028365

Book design and composition by Rita Lascaro
Typeset in Ingeborg

Manufactured in the United States of America. Printed on acid-free paper.

for us

CONTENTS

∽

"Are not the fine mixtures of red and white,
the expressions of every passion by greater or
less suffusions of colour in the one, preferable
to that eternal monotony, which reigns in the
countenances, that immovable veil of black which
covers all the emotions of the other race?"
　　　—Thomas Jefferson

"I had thereafter no desire to tear down that veil,
to creep through; I held all beyond it in common
contempt, and lived above it in a region of blue sky
and great wandering shadows."
　　　—W.E.B. Du Bois

BAD WEATHER

So used to drought, the city looked astonished
at the sky & I have to believe that's why

she didn't see me in the crosswalk. I was
on my way to celebrate another year

among my friends, then drowned by laughter
in an ambulance as it raced along

toward harbor. I used to fear my body
was a well anyone could toss

their wishes into, unbothered surface
pocked with light, so I'd be lying

if I said I didn't love it, the new storm,
minor catastrophe, me

in its mute eye. I leave the hospital & can't look
at anything. My skull wrung, wrong. Blessed din

of my solitary making, static song
no one else can hum along.

∽

Walking Lake Calhoun

to a.

In my favorite childhood memory

a blue lip of water is closing

above me & then my mother

is pulling me back up, though

she denies it. *You were never drowning*

she says. Love is no buoy.

This is as good a place as any

to begin, watching you descend

the stairs at 32nd St, back into my line

of sight. Here is the circle of my life

& here is yours, tangent extending

indefinitely away & here is the place

where, by definition, they always meet.

Rounding the bend, I almost tell you

but there's a monster rising

from the water that for years

killed off someone close to my heart—

massive jaws opening in the ocean

or sometimes, improbably,

appearing to fling the beloved

before a train—

What brought you here?

you're asking, Loch Ness statue

bobbing still, though out of sight.

What brought me here? My friends

& I live in one apartment building

& once a week drive to a diner uptown.

It's like being in a sitcom

about having friends, which is nice

because I never have to go outside.

Still, there are at least two worlds

in every person. Sometimes I look

too long at my friends' faces

& fall through the bottom

of our lifeboat & cannot find my way

back into the light & sure,

I'm the monster. Sure, I'm the one

eating my own heart.

My therapist would call this

a *cognitive distortion*, but I'm trying

to say that I prefer it, imagining myself

cruel & merely proximate to love.

Let me assure you I don't believe in us.

Not you & I, storied romance, grotesque

pronoun, *what am I without you?*

& here we are, back at the beginning.

We could walk another lap?

Not hug & say goodbye?

Though it isn't true, you know.

What I said before.

SOMETHING ABOUT JOY

I'm alone in this room
empty of me, though
I'm in it. The desk is full
of paper cups, still
with the residue of morning
coffee or afternoon coffee
or god, that which tethers me
to light. I'm not joking.
The joke is printed
on the cups, green
voice reassuring *You're*
Making A Difference!
because these cups
are compostable
these paper cups
bear the Earth
or at least its image
but I can't see
the forest from here
the blade descending
on a child skipping
out into the death field
to fill the cup I cradle
in my palm like a songbird.
Little joy & then it flies.

[BLACK FEELING]

after alton sterling

There's no logic to it, none
I can decipher.

Some mornings
silence, enough

I can pay attention, pace
around the internet

& nothing, no part
of my body

forces me to turn away.
On others, there's a dial

stuck inside, always
between stations

bad news / smooth jazz
& I can't turn it down

the blinding static.

On the internet
there are rooms

full of people
looking for a cure.

There are specialists
a diagnosis: *tinnitus*

from, of course, the Latin
tinnire, to ring

as in: a telephone
but there's no one home

to answer, no one
but me.

I imagine the hands
of whoever's calling, godlike

in their persistence
reaching out

down into my red
wiring—I'm sorry.

I don't mean to sound
ungrateful. I am grateful

as a weathervane
finally struck.

What strange
benevolence:

this morning, again
the country ablaze

firework / gunfire / man
of music & I

alone in the manic dark, head
in my hands ringing

& ringing, faithful
goddamned blood alarm.

ETYMOLOGY

Watching the video, again—

figures illuminated

by brutal choreography

men in costume & the other

thrashing, briefly

the dark heart

of cement & afterward

the law will claim

a breakdown—

He refused to follow

to comply I thought the gun

was real I thought

an adult nothing I could do

would stop him he looked

straight through me like

I wasn't even there

as a child

in America

you disregard

the wound of language

(how does it go?

sticks & stones?)

it isn't possible

a word might hurt you

might contain within itself

the red door in your boy's

head, opening

some nameless night

in every city... I know

I know, *don't shoot*

the messenger.

The dispatcher

just did her work.

Love Poem

In my worst years

I wanted you

to suffer

how I suffered

at every party

I hated

the idea of being

touched

could never

get used

to hours

with someone in them

I wanted

what? If I'm honest

I don't know

how to forgive

the animal you

broke inside me

always ruining the moment

with its wrecked imagination

I can't help

but think of you

Anti-Elegy

She was:

33, bullet.
35, bullet.
20, bullet.
25, stabbed to death & run over by a car.
66 blade.
22 bullet.
17 fist.
36 blade.
blade.
blade.
bullet.
bullet.
bullet
stone
found dead in a field
overdose
bullet
unknown
rope
stone
stone
bullet
oncoming traffic
his own good hands . . .

& it becomes a kind of music, doesn't it?
Senseless litany, field of roses, blood red
upturned skirts. I open my mouth & here,
the pith of me. Here, a flock of names, a girl
spilling out onto the street.

. . .

The trouble with elegy
is that it asks the dead

to live, it calls them back.
& who am I to say *rise?*

Walk again among those
who could not bear

the sight of you? Your body.
Your one good dress.

Today, someone will walk into the night
& then become it. Someone's heart

will crowd with beloved ghosts
& who am I to say, *dance*

with me here a little longer? Never mind
the bloodshed darling, never mind.

Never mind.

. . .

Once, a man said *mine*
& a woman became an empty room.

Once, a man said *mine*
& the ocean split & the endless passage.

Once, a man said *mine*
& there's a genocide—

how strange. To make the world
with language. To wield desire

as a weapon. To watch one nation burn
& another rise up at your feet.

Once, a girl looked in the mirror
& called herself, said *my name is*

said *I am / I am* & a man said
mine / mine / mine

. . .

I have so many questions:

Who are

What does

Why

How does it feel to

I'm sorry, I just think

I

And, define

I'm sorry

Your anger

You're afraid of

Can fear be

Define

knife

Define

Fear is

Please

Forgive

me

Meditations in an Emergency

I wake up & it breaks my heart. I draw the blinds
& the thrill of rain breaks my heart. I go outside.
I ride the train, walk among the buildings, men in
Monday suits. The flight of doves, the city of tents
beneath the underpass, the huddled mass, old
women hawking roses, & children all of them,
break my heart. There's a dream I have in which I
love the world. I run from end to end like fingers
through her hair. There are no borders, only wind.
Like you, I was born. Like you, I was raised in the
institution of dreaming. Hand on my heart. Hand
on my stupid heart.

∽

ALL MY FRIENDS ARE SAD & BRIGHT

I think *door* & there is. *Open* & here's a room
where everything you've lost is washed ashore.
We've seen the news. We know the story.
How even our bodies hurt us sometimes
so much. Room of broken mirrors. Room of salt.
Room of marigolds & it's your party, baby.
Here's a crown, here's a gown & no man
just around the corner, all your eyes on you.
I think *gunflower* & here's a field. Here's a room
where every bullet planted blooms. Boy with flower.
Boy with metal rose. What's done is done. What fire
fords you. I was a child once. Anything could be
my kingdom, all I had to do was say—
Here's a room of water & gold & nothing else.
A room in which a man takes back his blood.
Goodbye blood. Goodbye stars. Goodbye dead light
troubling the dance your body does all by itself.
I was by myself once, beside myself, breath
fogging up a window & what's on the other side?
Only everything you wanted & here's a room
of everything you wanted. Think *peppermint & myrrh*.
Think *loved* & you don't even have to die.

CARVE A SPACE TO HOLD OUR MOTHER

to my sister

Here, our father slams the door
on my fingers. Here he is
dancing with my feet
on his feet, *I'm so tired*
of being alone pulling us
across the room. Here
a flicker in every corner—
beige skirt draped
across the bed, red
robe hanging
like a skin. I'm sorry
for those years
I tried to feed you
to the dog, but who hasn't
fought to keep light
undivided?

. . .

Can a girl ever stand
far enough away
to see her mother
& not the edges
of a shadow bent
into her own?
Don't ask me
I'm not a girl
though I was
when I first saw her
body, doubled

& moving
down the hallway
beyond my door.

[BLACK FEELING]

Virtually, every Sunday, we gather
just the three of us: me, my sister,
the upper-right quadrant
of our mother's face.

It's nearly impossible to take
a disembodied forehead seriously
which is why, when my sister reveals
her girlfriend has left

because of the space sorrow rends
between them / the therapist
/ the raised dose, & mother you respond
kids these days are too reliant

on our false parachutes, well
you'll have to forgive how we laughed
& laughed, pealing like so many bells
calling the night home.

Oh, mother. It's been so long
since I was the girl in the kitchen
with the dull knife. So long mother
forgive me. It's just funny, you

had two daughters & then
you didn't & on the news or not
the world is ending, still, the world
of my kin not my kin

& I can't bear knowing there's a door
& behind the door a country
that loves my sisters, that tends
their gorgeous lives

& all they have to do is walk
from one dark into another boundless . . .
Mother, like anyone, I need help
raising the shroud

from my black shoulders, though I do
get it: the pills / Big Pharma / sham
crystalline coats / so what

if that's what lifts your children
here, fully to you?

My Little Sister Is in Love with a Girl Who Has Our Mother's Name

To d.

Don't bother. The punch line was here
before you walked into the room.

Something something Oedipus.
A father grows strange

to his family & a daughter
grows up to become him,

the other to become him.
Before, my sister was a dead-letter

girl, no mouth, or hands
where her mouth should be.

If she made no sound, it never
left her. Nothing left her.

She could be an emperor
if no one knew. That's a detail—

my sister training to reign in silence
for no reason of biology, unless

a person can be born with an orchid
in the throat, grief, a spare organ. No.

That isn't the right word. Never is,
not even to describe what happened

between us—my father & I—
when you built a world for me

he could not enter.

Essay on What Is & Isn't

to c.e.

When a man says *knife*
is no form of seduction

he means he's never been
split. But doesn't everyone

have a seam? Unravel
to dark sugar?

. . .

He tore a hole where there was
no hole, a dagger flat

against my tongue. Was it
violence? *Yes.* Also

I found a name then, became
stranger to everyone but me.

When a hole is open, anyone can use it.
I can cleave, push inside.

. . .

Once, I only ate what wouldn't
nourish. I had one mouth. Grew

thin as a wire.   Boy
in the beginning, a blade

severed the line, made you
a body & isn't that

when you learned hunger?

It's Important to Know What a "Man" "Is"

As a girl, enamored
with the fact of movement—

that I had arms to push against
the swelling tide—

I turned back only once
to see my parents, frantic

specks, as I fought to reach
the edge of this world

where even the sky
surrenders.

There's a version of the story
in which the sweet girl

never makes it home,
her lungs, unbraided

by salt. But because I did,
because I learned

the lesson, next time I slid
down the throat of a man,

I knew, kick

or not, what I was—
driftwood, kelp, glass

bottle. Moved through.
Spit up. So unlike the lover

who used to fish
me up from sleep,

fingers curled
into a hook I

thrashed around, gasping
for good air

until my love was satisfied.
You have to understand

the difference: it was my pleasure
she wanted, worst of all.

A MALE IMPERSONATOR.

Dora Trimble, a black female, who has been masquerading as a man under the alias of "Doc Edward," yesterday had to pay early for her masculine propensity. Dora did not like the frills and ruffles of femininity and the hundred other appendages of womankind that made her a prisoner of custom, so donning a pair of jeans, brogans, an elongated cap and other apparel usually worn by the sons of Adam, she paraded herself about as a man and a bully. She miscalculated the limit of her self-named privileges, and wandered into the domain of the bluecoat. So to speak, she was thereupon disrobed of her cunning character and turned over to Second Recorder Marmouget for disposition. The Recorder got rid of his charge in a few minutes. It was $10 or 20 days for Dora, and in default of payment of fine, she was given nine days additional board and lodging at the Parish Prison.

New Orleans Times-Picayune, November 25, 1903

[In the next room, wailing.
Man woman other can't tell.
Any human specificity obliterated
by pain. Someone walks
into the room where I am
pinned. Looks at me, my paperwork.
Backs away shaking his head]

       Doc

it

       has been
       yesterday

                    for
                    a   *hundred*

                        hundred

              days

        yesterday

      elongated

                 into

                                        a

Prison.

                                                           to

              day
                a black female,

                                           disrobed of

                              her

son

                    black
                                              dear

                                                        got

rid of

                                                        by

              black

appendages

                                                    of the
bluecoat.

   bully
              bluecoat.

          self-named privileges

          Doc

                                        days

turn   over

It
    has been
    yesterday

          i   *wander*   *the*
blue

      minutes

            disrobed

                        [As child, I too
                    was an impersonator.
                        I had a body
                        &, also, a life
                        that moved
                        with no regard
                        for form.

                        God willing, my will
                        carry me]

40

o

im

fine,

i   *m*

fine

[that long honeyed pause
between *I am* and *caught.*]

dear

prisoner

dear

                       alias

                        appendage

elongated

                   limit

parade

of

black

black

cunning

black

$

black

frill   and ruffle

dear

Doc

dear

other   i

dear

woman

man

self-named

Love Poem

Dear Proofreader,

you're right. It is warped.
My syntax, a sentence

on myself: third person
absent pronouns. I'm glad

you liked the article
about gender & interpretation.

Glad to grace your pages
wearing this ink

dress. Just what I wanted
I couldn't tell you

all those Christmas nights
of family, trying

to decipher their mutant
kin. Yes, I'm certain

the fault is mine. I
a fault line, been falling

through this fissure
all my life.

At the bottom of the problem?
[   ]

& at the bottom
of language, an animal

prayer & at the bottom of prayer
let me assure you

tangled fur, my proper name.

STONE DECEMBER

Except for the blue jay

jabbering for sex, solitary

bright note of sky. Except for

the wandering chickens

& the guard cats

the lone trees on my side

of the street still somehow

ablaze with fall. Except for this

whole animal world, I'll talk

to no one. No one.

Last night, with him

inside me I could remember why

I hate it. I wanted to say, *you have to*

make me ask for it but then

it was morning & he was

driving me back home. *Hush.*

How can I say this

so you'll believe me? *It's fine.*

It's all fine, perfect skein

of my living, brazen

misplaced song.

∽

[Black Feeling]

The white boy says to the white boi *you
say you think of your art as a public
service but you're underselling yourself
there's such discipline such stringent
rules* I carve in the margins HAVE
YOU EVER WORKED IN THE SERVICE
INDUSTRY dark voice inside me
standing at attention though I haven't
either worked in the service industry
I say nothing just roll my eyes in his
general direction without looking at
him at all the one magic trick I know
transform any statement to a barbed
face I show to no one now images of
black children rising against the world
is turning beside me a woman white in
red shawl gasps shakes her head she
can't believe it I can't believe when I
was a child like any child I understood
nothing *the idea of race* the white boi is
saying formed like a wall between me
& everyone once we were walking my
friend & I ugly with a rash where she
just days ago remade me in her image
I begged but now doesn't look at me
says we can't do this anymore she & I
because of the idea of race must have
been February when these things break
into the suburbs where we lived in
parallel but I swear there was so much
sun then suddenly

49

LOVE POEM

Dear woman, listening with your mouth
pursed into a false ear, which cannot—

despite the clarity with which my sisters,
who are poets, so precise

as an incision, describe how they are called
into the same work—

get over how both women tower
gracefully & both, of course, are black

so become, in your mouth, mother
& child, had to have shared a body,

been the same person. I suppose I'm grateful
when I can leave myself for long enough

to let a stranger or a love inside me, to be held
open as a tunnel for all the midnight traffic

or only you, whose face is not my face
until it is by some dark magic & oh, boy.

Dear dear boi. Whose body I slip into,
wear as a jacket against the rain.

Everyone Keeps Talking about Having Children

as if there is no drowning planet

no girl slipping beneath

her mother's skirt searching

for a door a neon exit

turn your head back

there's a world

on fire there's a ship dividing

un-navigable dark nothing

better there just different

horrors other endings

a silhouette tumbling

from the deck this way

at least she keeps

her name & why be reborn

why cast your line out

into the future tense

it's only another kind

of darkness promissory

sunrise if I must believe

in something it'll be

an invented physics I'll call it God

if I have to I'll shape a window

to the universe adjacent calm

my blackened heart imagine

instead this world

never had a chance.

AUBADE

The cat wakes me up as always
rooting her head between my chest
& chin & failing this, licks the lacy crud
hardening in the corners of my mouth
with her darling tongue, which she lets hang
between her lips as though ponderous
or posing for the camera, at least
when she's not using it to clean herself
from tail to toe to asshole & then my facehole,
which I know is a kind of favor—
after all, I'm hairless & ugly & too dumb
to lift my limbs from the bed & polish each one.
It's been so long, a whole season of drought
& what? You think I need to lift my head & pray
for rain? You think I need to twirl
beneath the firmament, the bruising sky?
& maybe you're right, or would be,
if I weren't half-boy, half-beast. If I didn't mark
these walls myself, slink around the furniture.
I confess, the cat is right. I do need help
keeping my face clean. Downy, these days
as a newborn. There's a reason, you know
we're all writers or gone, missing
from the world like we never happened
to have a skin, only some unhappy wind
passing through. I've lost you, haven't I?
But what can I say? I'm still right
here, haven't moved all morning & who could
be lonely when there's always this spectral self
to say hello to? Hello you. Darling you. Hello
sentry of my peace. Busy little tongue.

The Cure for What Ails You

is a good run, at least according to my mother,
which has seemed, all my life, like cruelty—

when I had a fever, for example, or a heart
shipwrecked & taking on the flood. But now,

of course, this is what I tell my friend whose eye
has been twitching since last Tuesday, what I

tell my student who can't seem to focus
her arguments, who believes, still

that it's possible to save the world
in 10-12 pages double-spaced, & without irony

I'm asking *Have you tried going for a run?*
You know, to clear your head? this mother-voice

drowning out what I once thought
to be my own. I'll admit that when that man

became the president, before terrified I felt
relief—finally, here was the bald face

of the country & now everyone had to look
at it. Everyone had to see what my loves,

for their lives, could not unsee. Cruelty
after all is made of distance—

sign here & the world ends
somewhere else. The world. The literal

world. I hold my face close to the blue
light of the screen until my head aches.

Until I'm sick & like a child I just want
someone to touch me with cool hands

& say *yes, you're right, something is wrong*
stay here in bed until the pain stops & Oh

mother, remember the night
when, convinced you were dying

you raced to the hospital clutching
your heart & by the time you arrived

you were fine. You were sharp
as a blade. Five miles in & I can't stop

thinking about that video. There's a man
with his arms raised

in surrender. He was driving
his car, his own car & they're charging him

bellowing like bulls *I didn't shoot you, motherfucker*
you should feel lucky for that. Yes. Okay.

Fine. My body too can be drawn
like any weapon.

STILL LIFE

to Lawrence Jackson, arrested in Chicago wearing a dress, 1881

A figure in the frame. Black dress slit
up the thigh, a voice issues from the seam.

I sit in the dark & watch your hips.
Your practiced walk.

. . .

Somewhere, there is a photograph
of me in a strapless dress. Me, flexing

my grin, my skinny arms. An image
won't show you the fight

at its edges—my girlfriend shining
like a pearl, her father's finger

on the shutter, the compromise
beneath the skirt.

. . .

If I can see you only in this moment
you are caught, what kind of we

does that make? Rows of dark bodies
hunched against the page, above

the page. In the archive of ink
& yellow trees, there you are

before the judge, offering to leave
the city, to walk away with nothing

in your pockets. No pockets.
This, you think, is what they want

from you. To look & not see you
standing.

. . .

What happens after that?
The trail ends with you, framed

by dark. They don't want us to leave,
exactly. Instead, to not have to look

to know we're there. Anything
can be made into a cage—

garment, sentence, cage.

. . .

I draw a frame around the frame,
a bright afternoon in Indiana

on your shoulders, dress
black & spun in a field of gold,

dress a knot of brazen black
birds, the body not a question.

BAD NEWS, AGAIN

after the June 2015 Charleston AME church shooting

There are so many reasons
to stay inside, to lock the room
around my heart. I don't even like it.
My heart. Bitter little fruit.
Little lead stone, carnation
blooming from a Sunday dress.
What does the world mean
if you can't trust it to go on?

. . .

Listen: birdsong (whippoorwill
maybe) broken by the wail
of a woman prowling barefoot
down the street.

. . .

Sometimes, before light breaks
I lace my shoes & race outside.
I try to touch everything—
my neighbor's rusty wind
chime, the fallen trees. My soles
drum the concrete, hands strum
each metal fence.

. . .

Listen: hasn't my body felt
like the body of smoke
before?

. . .

One morning, on the corner
a girl, still in plaits, crowned
with butterflies, a field that sang
with every motion of her head.
Where was her mother
at this hour? I don't know.

But she looked at me
like a child. She spun
her head. She laughed
& laughed at my awful music
& I thought Oh. Yes.
This is the world
with me in it. It is
beautiful. It is.

[BLACK FEELING]

. . .

&after that, even the whirring of your head goes quiet. Even your breath. No sound. Someone in workshop says something like, *in italian,* stanza *means* room. Don't roll your eyes. Here you are in the room. Here you are with things, but no names for things.

. . .

You've been in this city for weeks now & no one
knows your name. No one except the man at the
bus stop with his tallboy. His paper bag. When
he asks, you tell him you work at the university,
you teach. He was a cop, 'til someone died & he
found the bottle. Or, the drink came first &
then the falling off this umber world. In this
moment, you're a man to him. Some kind of
boy genius philosopher, who knows? There is
something neither one of you can say. You're
circling like animals, like prey.

. . .

The truth is, most black folk look at you & see
a woman. White people look at you & see a
reckless boy. Either way, there you are in the
room with your body.

. . .

Everywhere, the bus is a kind of underworld. The man lives there, but you are just a passenger. He clears a space, says *sit*. You can't sit. He looks at you with so much gratitude you think you'll die.

. . .

You have to understand that there are many rooms. Each of them operates by other laws. Here, once you name a thing, you can't take it back. It has its own life now, one that moves along without concern for you. At first, you go around talking to the trees & for just a moment they turn to face you.

. . .

By the time the bus arrives the light has gone &
the man is holding out his hand. You take it, not
expecting to be thrown against him. Against
him, you are years ago, a frantic girl alone. The
man is on his knees. You are a boy holding up
his brother. The man is on his knees. Either
way, there you are in the room with your body.
Your one, wet face.

[O
god of the loophole

god of the veil

of the break

the fugitive

in endless flight]

Somewhere, there's a room where things go to lose their names. A rose becomes [　]. A daughter becomes [　]. Her son [　].

. . .

Unlocking your apartment, you realize you never caught his name. He just looked at you & saw a door. He can't walk back through but there you were. An image racing on the other side.

∾

Cento Between the Ending and the End

Sometimes you don't die

when you're supposed to

& now I have a choice

repair a world or build

a new one inside my body

a white door opens

into a place queerly brimming

gold light so velvet-gold

it is like the world

hasn't happened

when I call out

all my friends are there

everyone we love

is still alive gathered

at the lakeside

like constellations

my honeyed kin

honeyed light

beneath the sky

a garden blue stalks

white buds the moon's

marble glow the fire

distant & flickering

the body whole bright-

winged brimming

with the hours

of the day beautiful

nameless planet. Oh

friends, my friends—

bloom how you must, wild

until we are free.

NOTES

"Something about Joy" takes its title from a poem by Dinah Fay of the same name.

"Etymology" borrows from the testimonies of Darren Wilson, Randall Kerrick, and Frank Garmback, officers not convicted for killing Michael Brown, Jonathan Ferrel, and Tamir Rice, respectively.

"Love Poem [In my worst years]" borrows a line from Jason Shinder.

"Meditations in an Emergency" is in conversation with Frank O'Hara's poem of the same name.

"All my friends are sad & bright" rewrites Richard Siken's "Snow and Dirty Rain" and borrows from Danez Smith.

"Bad News, Again" rewrites Mary Oliver's "October."

"Cento Between the Ending and the End" is composed of language scavenged from the work of: Justin Phillip Reed, Hieu Minh Nguyen, Fatimah Asghar, Kaveh Akbar, Sam Sax, Ari Banias, C. Bain, Oliver Bendorf, Hanif Abdurraqib, Safia Elhio, Danez Smith, Ocean Vuong, Franny Choi, Lucille Clifton, and Nate Marshall.

ACKNOWLEDGMENTS

Many thanks to the editors of the following journals for first publishing poems included in this collection, often in slightly different forms: *The Shade Journal, Bat City Review, TheThePoetry, Drunken Boat* (now *ANMLY*), *Hayden's Ferry Review, The Baffler, Narrative, Indiana Review, Vetch, BOAAT, Narrative Northeast, American Poetry Review, Academy of American Poets Poem-a-Day,* and *The Rumpus.*

"The Cure for What Ails You" appears in *Nepantla: An Anthology Dedicated to Queer Poets of Color,* "[Black Feeling] the white boy says . . ." appears in *Bettering American Poetry vol. 2,* and "Still Life" appears in *Subject to Change: Trans Poetry and Conversation.* Thanks to the editors of these anthologies for giving these poems their second homes.

Also, of course, many, many thanks to Gabriel Fried and everyone at Persea for believing in this little book and in me, for giving my work a home and wonderful company.

I began writing this book at Cave Canem and completed it at The Watering Hole. My endless gratitude to all of the staff, faculty, and fellows that make these spaces for black/poc poetry possible and full. Thanks, in particular, to Nicole Sealey, Toi Derricotte, Cornelius Eady, Monifa Lemons, Candace G. Wiley, Terrance Hayes, Amber Flora Thomas, Lyrae Van Clief-Stefanon, Evie Shockley, Willie Perdomo, and Chris Abani.

Further, this book would not exist if not for so many people whose writing and living makes mine possible, whether they know it or not: Fatimah Asghar, Nate Marshall, Hanif Abdurraqib, Paul Tran, Jamila Woods, Justin Phillip Reed, Cass Adair, Kaveh Akbar, Paige Lewis, Safia Elhillo, Angel Nafis, Shira Erlichman, Alison C. Rollins, Joy Ladin, TC Tolbert, etc. etc. etc.

To my parents for giving me all the tools I needed to build the life I have, the life I wanted, and then turning me loose; to my sister for being my hype-man, my constant, my friend; and to Sonia, David, and Lauren for their happy years – thank you, thank you, thank you.

To Nick, for a good year, for petitioning the stars on my behalf, for keeping me tethered.

To Sam, Hieu, and Danez, who are with me always, even and especially when I have vanished into myself – it's all because of you.

Finally, to you, Frances. For everything, but most of all for making it all the way to the uncharted inner room and choosing me anyway. How unspeakably lucky.